Eastern Mediterranean Region

Last Updated: August 15, 2013 (Notes)
full report

Overview of oil and natural gas in the Eastern Mediterranean region

Offshore natural gas discoveries in the Levant Basin have the potential to significantly alter energy supply dynamics in the eastern Mediterranean region, however several outstanding issues—including armed conflict, territorial disputes, and macroeconomic uncertainty—could limit the viability of those supplies in the short term.

The eastern Mediterranean region—defined in this report as Cyprus, Israel, Jordan, Lebanon, Syria, and the Palestinian Territories—is currently undergoing changes to its energy landscape. With expected economic growth, and the population of the region forecast to grow from 45.3 million in 2010 to between 58 and 62 million in 2030[1], energy demand should increase noticeably over the next two decades. At present levels of consumption, regional oil and natural gas reserves are unlikely to last for more than a few decades. Fortunately, recent discoveries of large hydrocarbon resources—particularly natural gas—in the offshore Levant Basin significantly alter the supply-side forecasts for the region. These discoveries have the potential to provide the necessary energy supply to meet growing regional demand and possibly even spur exports.

There are several issues facing the region that could significantly affect how quickly and how successfully such changes occur. Among the major issues in the region, physical and economic security as well as offshore hydrocarbon development will have the most influence on the region's energy sector. Unrest in Syria and Egypt and territorial disputes between several of the countries in the eastern Mediterranean will impact regional energy production, consumption, and trade. Further, negative economic developments in the region —influenced by issues such as the Cyprus debt crisis and the war in Syria—could undermine demand, interrupt production and trade, and threaten the viability of several energy infrastructure projects. Overcoming these challenges is critical to the success of the region's energy future.

History

The hydrocarbons sector began developing in the eastern Mediterranean approximately 80 years ago when oil exploration began in Syria following the successes in neighboring countries such as Saudi Arabia. Commercial oil production in Syria did not begin in earnest until the 1960s, while oil exploration activities in Israel and Jordan ramped up in the 1960s and 1970s, although with far less success than in Syria. Nevertheless, production at very low levels persists in both Israel and Jordan. Both Syria and Israel are also natural gas producers, although those sectors did not develop commercially until the 1980s in Syria and the mid-2000s in Israel. Jordan has had very low levels of production of both oil and natural gas since the 1980s, and the country relies primarily on imports to meet internal demand. In Cyprus, Lebanon, and the Palestinian Territories oil exploration and development is still in its infancy, however each hopes to capitalize on successful offshore exploration in the Levant Basin to develop domestic natural gas resources.

Efforts to move energy resources through the eastern Mediterranean region, located between the major supply countries in the Middle East and major demand centers in Europe, have been ongoing for decades. Even before beginning oil and natural gas operations of their own in the 1960s and 1970s, eastern Mediterranean countries—notably Syria—often benefitted from transit fees paid to them by nearby exporters like Iraq and Saudi Arabia. Today, there is considerable focus on exploration and new projects, but international transit remains a key policy consideration of several eastern Mediterranean countries. As the region continues to discover and develop hydrocarbon resources, the pressure to increase its role as an important energy hub is likely to increase.

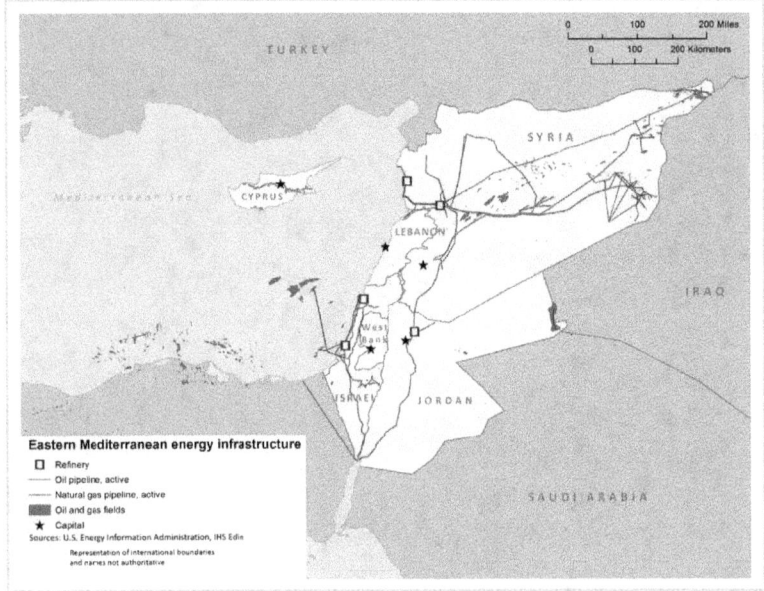

Eastern Mediterranean energy infrastructure
▫ Refinery
— Oil pipeline, active
— Natural gas pipeline, active
▪ Oil and gas fields
★ Capital
Sources: U.S. Energy Information Administration, IHS Edin
Representation of international boundaries
and names not authoritative

Geology

While most of the historical production in the eastern Mediterranean countries came from the Western Arabian Province and the Zagros Province, the Levant Basin is the center of most of the recent exploration activities in the region.

The eastern Mediterranean region includes eight significant basins (Cyprus basin, Eratosthenes High, Latakia basin, Levant basin, Judea basin, Nile Delta basin, Western Arabian province, and Zagros province), with the majority of the historical hydrocarbon production occurring in the Nile Delta Basin, the Western Arabian Province, and the Zagros Province. Most of the Nile Delta Basin lies within Egypt's territorial waters, although there is a small area under Cypriot control. To date, there have not been any significant discoveries in the Cypriot territory, although much of Egypt's offshore oil and gas production comes from the area. The Western Arabian province basin covers large parts of Jordan and Syria, and extends into Iraq, Saudi Arabia, and Turkey. Most of Jordan's fields and many of Syria's are in the Western Arabian Province. The Zagros Province extends from Turkey in the north, through Iraq and Iran, terminating in the Gulf of Oman in the south. Several of Syria's largest fields are part of the Zagros Province, but the vast majority of fields in the Zagros Province are in other countries including Iraq, Iran, and Saudi Arabia. While the Western Arabian and

Zagros Provinces account for most of the historical hydrocarbon production in the region, most of the focus today is on the Levant Basin.

Levant Basin

Extending across a large section of the offshore areas of the eastern Mediterranean, the Levant Basin is at the center of recent energy exploration in the region. In a 2010 report, the U.S. Geological Survey (USGS) estimated that the Levant Basin has mean probable undiscovered[2] oil resources of 1.7 billion barrels and, more significantly, mean probable undiscovered natural gas resources of 122 trillion cubic feet (Tcf). In context, the combined proved reserves of oil in the countries included in this report totaled just over 2.5 billion barrels as of January 2013—99.5 percent of which belong to Syria—and proved natural gas reserves of 18.2 Tcf. The USGS also estimated the mean probable undiscovered resources of natural gas liquids (NGL) at 3.1 billion barrels.

While the USGS estimates do not reflect the entirety of potential energy resources in the eastern Mediterranean region, the resources of the Levant Basin likely represent a large part of the overall resource base. The USGS estimate of 1.7 billion barrels of oil, if discovered, would increase the region's proved reserves by slightly less than 70 percent, while the 122 Tcf of natural gas represents more than six times the region's current proved reserves. An additional 1.7 billion barrels of oil in the Levant Basin would meet regional demand for roughly 20 years at current levels of consumption, while 122 Tcf of natural gas could meet current regional demand almost indefinitely. Nearly all the recent significant discoveries in the Levant Basin were of natural gas, and, while offshore exploration may eventually yield recoverable quantities of oil, to date there have not been any commercially-viable discoveries.

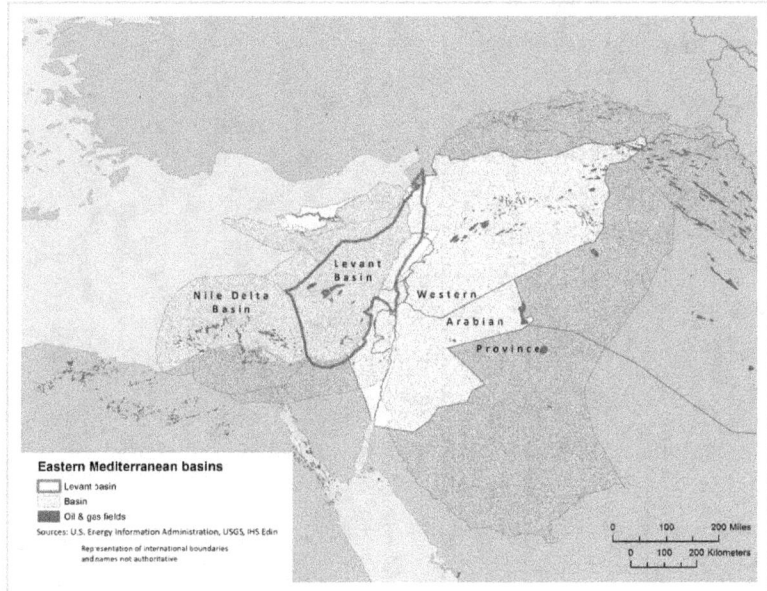

Reserves and recent discoveries

As of January 2013, the largest reserves of oil in the eastern Mediterranean region belonged to Syria, while recent discoveries of natural gas gave Israel the largest proved reserves of natural gas.

Proved reserves of oil and natural gas

In a global context, the energy resources of the eastern Mediterranean represent less than 1 percent of the world's total proven reserves of oil and natural gas.

The combined proved reserves of oil in the countries covered in this report—slightly more than 2.5 billion barrels—are far less than found in other nearby regions, such as Mediterranean North Africa[3] (65 billion barrels) based on *Oil & Gas Journal* figures for 2013. Syria holds the largest proved reserves of oil of the countries covered in this report, but it ranks just 32nd in the world.

Like oil, current natural gas reserves in the eastern Mediterranean are relatively insignificant on a global scale. As of January 2013, the *Oil & Gas Journal* estimated the total combined proved reserves of natural gas in the countries covered by this report at 18.2 Tcf. By comparison, nearby Mediterranean North African countries hold approximately 239 Tcf in combined proved reserves of natural gas according to the *Oil & Gas Journal* as of 2013. While the total combined proved reserves of natural gas in the eastern Mediterranean are insignificant relative to global levels, recent discoveries in the offshore waters of Cyprus and Israel in the Levant Basin pushed the estimated recoverable natural gas resources in the area to over 38 Tcf.

Syria possesses the largest proved reserves of crude oil in the eastern Mediterranean countries. The *Oil & Gas Journal* estimated Syria's proved reserves at 2.5 billion barrels in January 2013, a total larger than all of Syria's neighbors except for Iraq. The *Oil & Gas Journal* also reported at the end of 2012 that Syria held proved reserves of 8.5 Tcf of natural gas. This gives Syria the largest conventional hydrocarbon resource base of the countries in this report, although the recent discoveries in neighboring Israel mean that this could change at some point in the future.

Large discoveries of natural gas in Israel's offshore areas prompted increased interest in the country's hydrocarbon sector, although to date there have not been any large commercially-viable oil discoveries. On the other hand, the changes in Israel's natural gas sector since 2000 have been immense. In 2000, the *Oil & Gas Journal* estimated that Israel held proved reserves of natural gas totaling just 10 billion cubic feet (Bcf). As of January 2013, that total was 9.5 Tcf, with recent offshore discoveries likely to boost that figure even higher.

Of the other countries in the region, Jordan—unlike several of its neighbors—does not possess significant oil resources and holds just 213 Bcf in proved reserves of natural gas according to the Oil & Gas Journal. Cyprus, Lebanon, and the Palestinian Territories did not have significant proved reserves of oil or natural gas as of January 2013, according to the Oil & Gas Journal, but successful offshore exploration in the Levant Basin over the past several years means that the level of reserves should soon change in Cyprus and the Palestinian Territories. Further, planned exploration in Lebanon could uncover recoverable quantities of oil and natural gas in the coming years.

Recent natural gas discoveries in the eastern Mediterranean region

Discovery	Field	Estimated reserves	First

Country	date	name	(Tcf)	volumes
Cyprus	2011	Aphrodite	7	2017
Israel	1999	Noa	0.04	2012
	2000	Mari-B	1.5	2004
	2009	Dalit	0.5	2013
	2009	Tamar	10	2013
	2010	Leviathan	18	2016
	2011	Dolphin	0.08	unknown
	2012	Shimshon	0.3	unknown
	2012	Tanin	1.2	unknown
	2013	Karish	1.8	unknown
Palestinian Territories	2000	Gaza Marine	1	unknown

Source: EIA estimates, IHS, Oxford Institute for Energy Studies, Oil & Gas Journal, company reports, trade press

Offshore exploration and discoveries

The recent natural gas discoveries in Cyprus and Israel have sparked increased interest in the potential energy resources contained in the offshore Levant Basin.

Recent natural gas discoveries in the Levant Basin have significantly altered the energy outlook in the eastern Mediterranean. Success in Israel, Cyprus, and the Palestinian Territories, spurred additional exploration in the region, and Lebanon and Syria both hope to launch exploration programs soon. Lebanon's exploration is in the early stages of licensing, but exploration in Syria is postponed indefinitely. The influence of the Syrian conflict, territorial disputes, and the economies of the countries in the region will influence the scale and success of exploration activities.

Of the significant natural gas fields discovered over the past decade, almost all have been in the Levant Basin. Most were in Israel's territorial waters, although there were significant discoveries in Cyprus and the Palestinian Territories as well. Exploration in Lebanon and Jordan continues, however there have not been any large commercial discoveries as of June 2013. Syria, previously the region's primary hydrocarbon producer, is unlikely to move forward with exploration projects as long as the conflict between government and opposition forces persists. Nevertheless, the exploration successes in Cyprus and Israel, and to a lesser degree the Palestinian Territories, have shown the potential for offshore energy production, especially natural gas production, in the eastern Mediterranean.

The discovery of the Noa field in 1999 and the Mari-B field in 2000 and discoveries in 2009 (Dalit and Tamar), 2010 (Leviathan), and 2011 (Aphrodite and Tanin) by U.S. firm Noble Energy confirmed the presence of significant quantities of natural gas in the Levant Basin. The largest offshore discovery in the eastern Mediterranean to date is the Leviathan field—located approximately 80 miles off the coast of Israel and situated in water that is more than 5,000 feet deep—which holds 18 Tcf in estimated recoverable resources. There are plans to drill exploratory oil wells below the offshore Leviathan gas field sometime in 2013, as some estimates indicate there could be up to 600 million barrels of oil located in the field as well.

Another significant Israeli find, the Tamar field, began operations in April 2013, and the Dalit and Tanin fields should come online sometime in the next decade. Recent revisions to resource estimates for the Tamar field brought the estimated recoverable reserves to 10 Tcf, enough to meet present levels of Israel's demand for decades. The Tamar field started production in a surprisingly short period of time, with less than five years between the discovery and commercially-viable production.

In addition to the discoveries in Israel, Cyprus has also had successful exploration in its offshore territory. Thus far, the most notable natural gas discovery in Cypriot waters was the Aphrodite field in Block 12 made by Noble Energy in 2011, estimated to contain 7 Tcf of natural gas. Noble Energy—the company behind most of the major natural gas discoveries in the region—began drilling its second well in Block 12 in June 2013. Government officials aim to capitalize on the exploration success in Block 12 to pursue additional resources in Cypriot waters, and hope to discover between 30 and 40 Tcf of additional natural gas. A bidding round for several of the country's offshore blocks closed in 2012, with awards going to a diverse group of international companies and consortia. Italian company Eni and South Korean company Korean Gas Corporation (KOGAS) won the bid for blocks 2, 3, and 9, while the French firm Total came away with Blocks 10 and 11.

Another potentially significant find in the Levant Basin is the Aphrodite-2 well, on the Israeli side of the maritime boundary with Cyprus. The Aphrodite-2 natural gas could be part of the same geologic structure as Cyprus' Aphrodite field and may have over 3 Tcf of technically recoverable resources. Should the Aphrodite-2 prove to be a part of the same structure as Cyprus' field, the two countries will need to negotiate a utilization agreement before production begins.

Similarly, exploration in the area straddling the maritime boundary between Israel and the Palestinian Territories indicates that there are potentially significant quantities of hydrocarbons in the area. The Gaza Marine field holds an estimated 1 Tcf in recoverable resources, and in September 2012, the Palestinian Authority and Israel discussed developing the offshore Gaza territory, although no firm agreements are in place. Additionally, Israel's Meged wells (onshore) and Noa field (offshore) showed promise earlier this decade, and both are close to the assumed Israel-Palestinian Territories boundary. Proved and probable reserves at the Meged field—discovered in 2004 by Givot Olam Oil Exploration—are in excess of 10 million barrels, and they may extend into Palestinian territory.

The government of Lebanon completed a pre-qualification bid for exploration in the country's territorial waters in April 2013. Fifty-two companies applied for pre-qualification, and 46 of those had their applications accepted. The formal licensing round began in May 2013, and bidding should conclude by the end of November 2013, with awards announced in February 2014. Barring any further delays, development work could begin by 2016. In February 2013, industry sources indicated that the Lebanese government would allow energy companies to operate in the country without Lebanese partners (previously, companies operated in conjunction with state-led companies), but details on such matters—as well as on the size and number of blocks up for bid—are scarce.

Early estimates of Lebanon's offshore reserve potential range into the hundreds of millions of barrels of oil, and Lebanon's government estimates that there are potential natural gas resources of 25 Tcf located in its offshore territory. Early seismic results indicate that resources in the southern sector of Lebanon's exclusive economic zone (EEZ) could total 12 Tcf, but confirmation of these estimates requires additional study.

Energy exploration in Syria, already limited, is at a virtual standstill as a result of the ongoing conflict in the country. A bidding round for offshore blocks was to conclude in 2011, but the government postponed the awards, and, as long as the current conflict persists, additional bidding rounds are unlikely to occur. After several delays, the blocks finally went to tender in December 2011. However, Syria has not announced the results as of July 2013. Syria reportedly held discussions with international partners—notably Russia and China—on further exploration in the country's offshore territory in April 2013, but details remain scarce.

Onshore exploration and discoveries

Onshore exploration for oil and natural gas is ongoing in several of the eastern Mediterranean countries, although not to the same degree as the offshore exploration.

The conflict in Syria limits the ability and desire of companies to operate in that country, as most of the international oil companies abandoned their operations in the country as the violence escalated over the past few years and as sanctions targeting Syria's energy sector came into effect. There is some onshore exploration in Israel, with some moderate success at wells in the eastern areas of the country. Recently Israel also moved ahead with exploration in the disputed Golan Heights region—which both Israel and Syria claim—awarding a drilling contract in February 2012. Exploration for hydrocarbons is proceeding slowly in Jordan, but several major international energy companies have interests in the country. Based on the results of exploration to date, areas near Jordan's eastern border with Iraq and around the Dead Sea could contain additional resources, but there have not been any major discoveries announced.

There is limited onshore exploration in Cyprus, Lebanon, and the Palestinian Territories. In total, with the current security environment in Syria and the limited efforts in the other countries of the eastern Mediterranean, most of the exploration in the near term will be focused on the offshore areas of the Mediterranean Sea.

Oil shale, shale oil, and other resources

Shale oil and oil shale resources have the potential to boost eastern Mediterranean oil reserves, but commercial production is likely still a few years away.

Several eastern Mediterranean countries possess other energy resources—including oil shale and shale oil—in addition to conventional oil and natural gas resources, but commercial production from any of these sources is likely still years away. With most exploration in the broader region focusing on the emerging Levant Basin, unconventional energy resources have not developed to the same extent that they have elsewhere in the world.

Israel has oil shale resources, but they have not been in production for some time. In the late 1980's an electric power plant opened that used oil shale, but it is no longer operating. In 2008, Israel Energy Initiatives (IEI) received a license to begin early stages of exploration and development of Israel's oil shale, and the company hopes to begin operating a 2,000 bbl/d demonstration site some time before 2020. The USGS reported in 2005 that Israel's oil shale deposits may total 12 billion tons.

Syria also has oil shale resources, with estimates of reserves ranging as high as 50 billion tons according to Syrian government sources in late 2010. However, instability in the country prompted officials to delay a bidding round for the county's oil shale resources, previously scheduled for November 2011. With the ongoing fighting and the current sanctions imposed on the Syrian energy sector by the United States, European Union, and others, international energy companies may find it difficult to operate in the country. Given those difficulties, and the higher cost of developing unconventional hydrocarbons relative to conventional hydrocarbons, additional progress in Syria is unlikely in the near term.

Jordan, like both Israel and Syria, also has oil shale deposits. According to the USGS, Jordan's oil shale resources total nearly 65 billion tons. These resources, should they prove economically viable, could help Jordan reduce its dependence on foreign energy sources at some point in the future. In addition to the country's oil shale deposits, a report released by the U.S. Energy Information Administration in June 2013 indicated that Jordan possesses 1.5 million barrels of technically recoverable shale oil resources and 6.9 Tcf of technically recoverable natural gas resources. As of early 2013 such resources are not yet commercially viable.

Regional oil and natural gas production and consumption

Most of the current production of oil and natural gas in the eastern Mediterranean is in Israel and Syria, which together account for 99 percent of all oil and natural gas production in the region.

Oil and natural gas reserves, production, and consumption

Country	Proved reserves, 2013 (billion barrels)	Total oil supply, 2012 (thousand barrels per day)	Total petroleum consumption, 2012 (thousand barrels per day)	Proved reserves, 2013 (trillion cubic feet)	Dry production, 2011 (billion cubic feet)	Consumption, 2011 (billion cubic feet)
Cyprus	--	0.01	60.04	--	--	--
Israel	0.01	5.84	301.65	9.48	91.82	117.25
Jordan	(s)	0.16	108.61	0.21	8.12	37.43
Lebanon	--	--	104.86	--	--	--
Palestinian Territories	--	--	23.26	--	--	--
Syria	2.50	182.46	257.65	8.50	277.93	286.76
Total, Region	*2.51*	*188.47*	*856.07*	*18.20*	*377.87*	*441.44*

Total oil supply includes crude oil, condensates, natural gas plant liquids, refinery processing gain, and other liquids

(s) = Value is too small for the number of decimal places

"--" = No value

Source: U.S. Energy Information Administration

Syria has historically been a relatively important producer—particularly relative to its non-OPEC neighbors—but the conflict that began in March 2011 is severely limiting its ability to produce (and export) petroleum supplies. That conflict and the unrest in Egypt that also began in 2011 have dramatically altered the energy outlook for the region, as Syrian oil and natural gas production continues to drop, and natural gas flows from Egypt—a key source of natural gas to the region—declined dramatically. Israel is the only other eastern Mediterranean country with significant hydrocarbon production (natural gas), although developments in the Levant Basin and elsewhere could alter the outlook for several countries in the region.

To meet expected rising demand, countries in the region will need to either produce or import additional energy supplies. Israel's successful development of offshore natural gas fields significantly altered its energy profile, as the country now projects to meet internal natural gas demand for years. Those volumes will also help it reduce petroleum consumption. Other countries in the region hope to follow suit, but progress has been uneven. If they are unable to produce oil or natural gas domestically, those countries will need to import energy supplies from outside the region. With unrest in nearby suppliers like Iraq and Egypt, procuring such supplies may prove difficult.

Syria is the region's only significant oil producer, but it is not a major supplier to other countries in the region at this time. Significant gaps between regional oil production and oil consumption totals indicate that the region requires high levels of petroleum imports to satisfy demand. In addition, the reserves to production ratio indicates that there is only enough economically recoverable oil presently available to maintain current production rates for 20 years. If regional consumption patterns shift away from imports towards the use of more local resources, the region will be self-sufficient for less than 10 years given current levels of proved reserves. Of course, imports, exports, the availability and viability of unconventional resources, changing demand patterns, and new discoveries will all combine to change supply dynamics in the region.

The eastern Mediterranean region's natural gas market continues to mature, and even without additional exploration and development the region's reserves are enough to meet current demand levels for over 40 years. In 2011, the combined dry natural gas production in the eastern Mediterranean was 378 Bcf, while total consumption was 441 Bcf. Israel and Syria accounted for nearly all of the region's gross production and 92 percent of its consumption. Recent declines in Syrian natural gas production due to instability in the country will be partly offset by growth elsewhere in the region, especially in Cyprus and Israel where a number of recent discoveries should come on-line in the coming years. Regional natural gas consumption dropped by 23 percent between 2010 and 2011, from 571 Bcf to 441 Bcf. This 23-percent decline came largely as a result of interruptions in flows from Egypt (which previously exported natural gas to Israel, Jordan, Lebanon, and Syria) and the onset of violence in Syria.

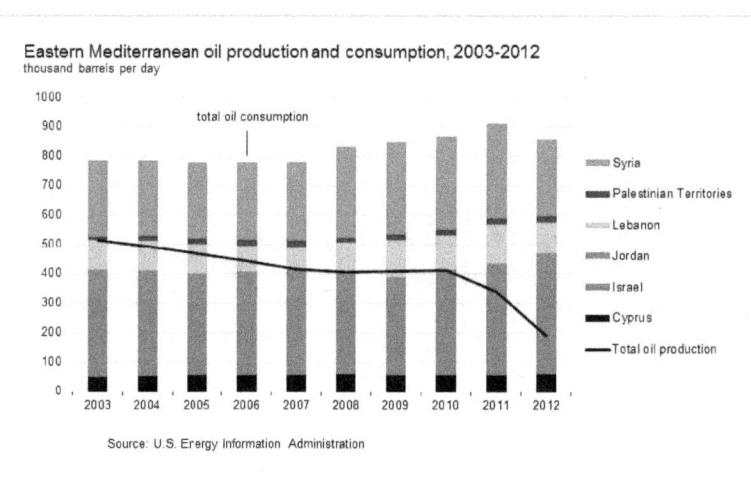

Eastern Mediterranean oil production and consumption, 2003-2012
thousand barrels per day

Source: U.S. Energy Information Administration

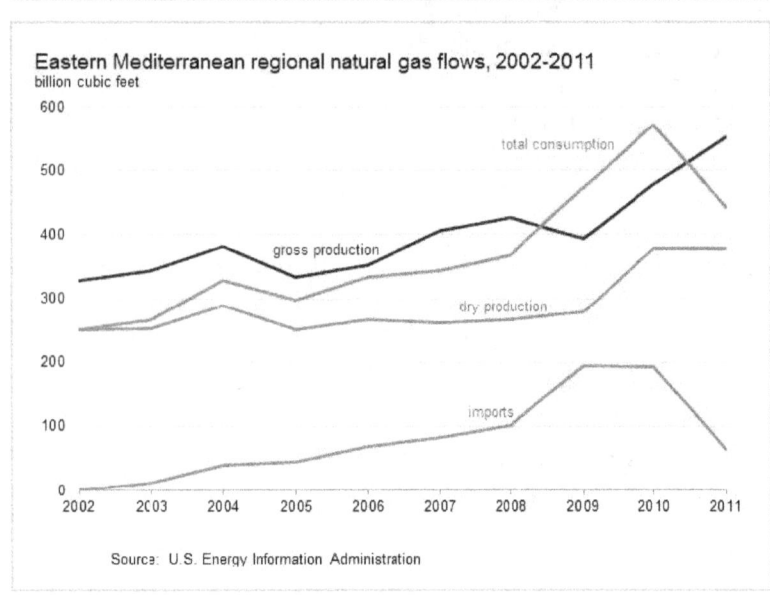

Eastern Mediterranean regional natural gas flows, 2002-2011
billion cubic feet

Source: U.S. Energy Information Administration

Syria

View the full Country Analysis Brief for Syria

Energy exploration and production in Syria began to fall with the onset of unrest in 2011, but the country continues to do its best to maximize its output in the face of stiff sanctions and damage to its energy infrastructure. Even when the fighting subsides, it may take many months—or years—for the Syrian domestic energy sector to return to pre-conflict operating status. The majority of Syria's oil and natural gas fields are in the central and eastern parts of the country near the border with Iraq, and they have increasingly come under threat as the conflict in Syria persists. Most of Syria's fields are no longer under the control of the forces supporting Bashar al-Assad, and, according to government officials, regime-controlled production stood at just 20,000 bbl/d in June 2013.

Average Syrian oil production from 2006-2010 was approximately 411,000 barrels per day (bbl/d) but declined steadily throughout that period. Due to the combination of military conflict and economic sanctions, average production slowed considerably, dropping from 380,000 bbl/d in March 2011 to 117,000 bbl/d in March 2013, a nearly 70-percent decline from pre-conflict levels. Even before 2011, Syria was not able to produce enough petroleum products to satisfy its demand. In 2011, Syrian total petroleum consumption was 258,000 bbl/d while total production was 330,800 bbl/d, but the country had limited refining capacity and had to import refined products.

Prior to 2011, Syria planned to expand its natural gas activities in an effort to help ease the demand for petroleum products. Most of Syria's natural gas is used by commercial and residential customers and in power generation, but Syria also uses its natural gas in oil-recovery efforts, with an average of nearly 17 percent of daily gross production re-injected into the country's oil fields between 2000 and 2011. In 2010, the last year under normal operating conditions, Syria produced 316 billion cubic feet (Bcf) of dry natural gas. In 2011, that figure fell by 12 percent to 278 Bcf. While data for 2012 are currently unavailable, natural gas production volumes should be even lower than 2011, as the combination of damaged infrastructure and reduced oil production (which uses substantial volumes of natural gas in recovery operations) combined to undermine domestic demand for natural gas.

In 2008, Syria became a net importer of natural gas, but the country's current security situation—and the attendant sanctions—could impact the ability of Syria to receive volumes in the future. Syria's plans to convert all existing thermal power generation facilities to natural gas-fired plants (many are currently using refined petroleum products) hinge on these volumes of natural gas being available, but this paln appears out of reach, at least in the short term.

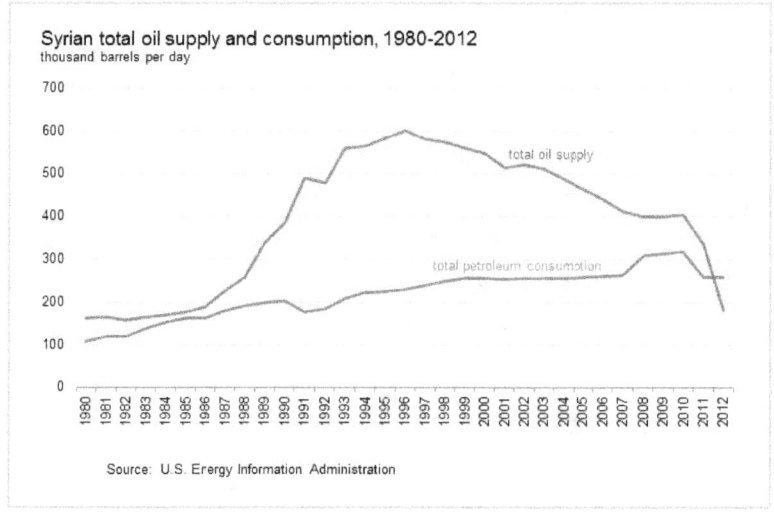

Syrian total oil supply and consumption, 1980-2012
thousand barrels per day

Source: U.S. Energy Information Administration

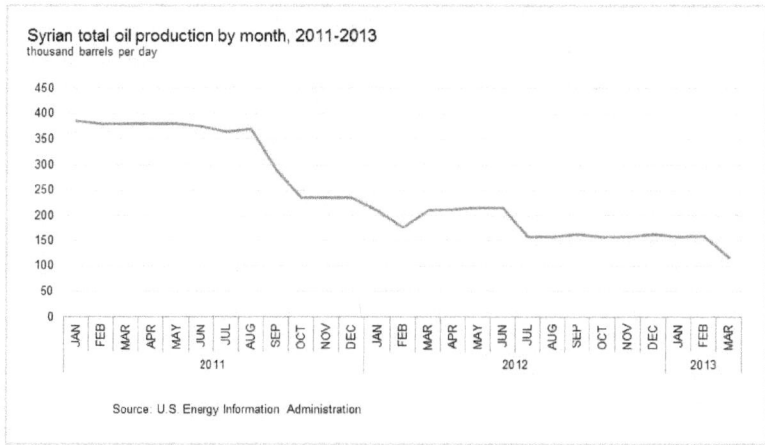

Syrian total oil production by month, 2011-2013
thousand barrels per day

Source: U.S. Energy Information Administration

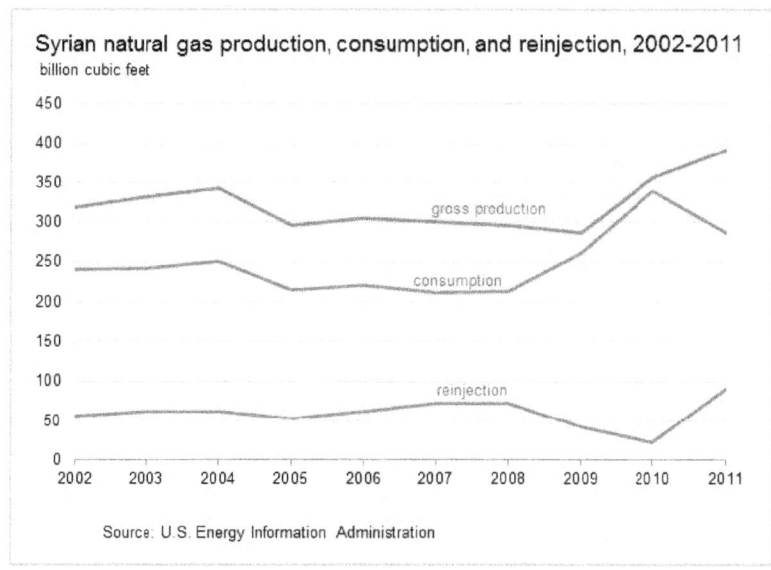

Syrian natural gas production, consumption, and reinjection, 2002-2011
billion cubic feet

Source: U.S. Energy Information Administration

Israel

While not a significant oil producer like Syria, Israel is the eastern Mediterranean's largest consumer of petroleum. Total Israeli oil consumption averaged 246,000 bbl/d from 2000-

2011, ranging from a low of 233,000 bbl/d in 2005 to a high of 263,000 bbl/d in 2011. In addition, Israel was the region's second-largest natural gas consumer in 2011, the last year for which EIA data are available. Unlike Israel's petroleum consumption—which Israel meets with imports—much of the natural gas consumed in Israel over the last decade came from domestic sources. Israel wants to increase the utilization of natural gas across all end-use sectors. However, even with increased demand Israel should have more than enough domestically-produced natural gas to meet its growing needs, and the country could begin exporting volumes as soon as 2017.

The Mari-B field—discovered in 2000—provided the first significant volumes of domestically-produced natural gas to Israel's markets, but in 2012 production plummeted as the field entered the final stages of depletion. In prior years, the Mari-B field met up to 40 percent of Israel's natural gas demand. Israel's total production volumes in 2012 reached more than 150 Bcf, after being as low as 350 million cubic feet (MMcf) as recently as 2002. Natural gas consumption in Israel also grew in recent years, from an annual average of 350 MMcf between 2000 and 2002 to a peak of 129 Bcf in 2010.

With additional production volumes coming online from the Tamar field in early 2013, the domestic market should continue to shift away from other energy sources in favor of natural gas. Existing infrastructure at the Mari-B development site moves the natural gas produced from the Tamar field to onshore facilities at the Ashdod terminal, with initial volumes of 500 MMcf/d and peak flow rates of up to 1 billion cubic feet per day (Bcf/d) in the near future. Natural gas for Israeli domestic use from the Leviathan field could be ready as soon as 2016, and it should begin with productive volumes of up to 750 MMcf/d.

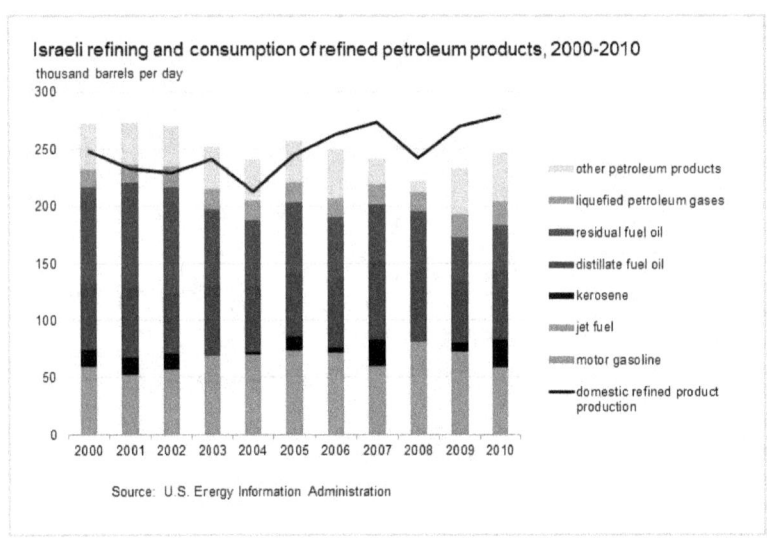

Israeli refining and consumption of refined petroleum products, 2000-2010

Source: U.S. Energy Information Administration

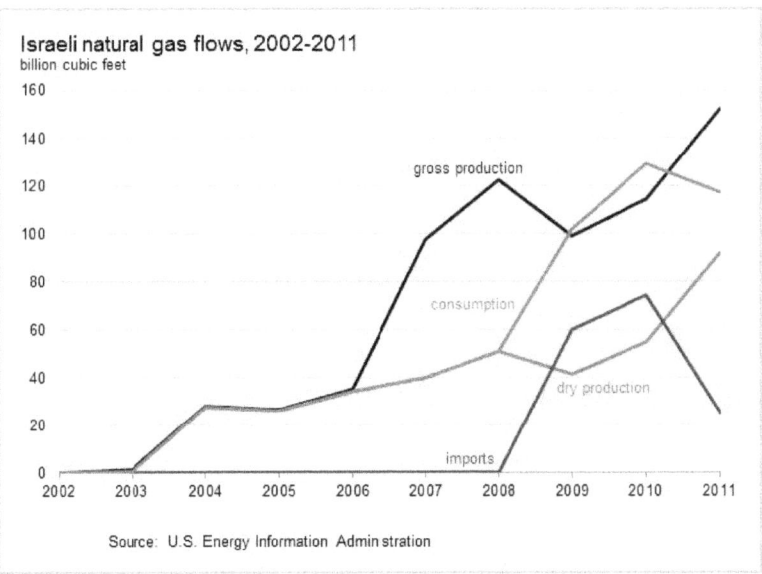

Israeli natural gas flows, 2002-2011
billion cubic feet

Source: U.S. Energy Information Administration

Cyprus

Like Israel, Cyprus hopes that its recent discoveries will allow for substitution away from petroleum products towards utilizing more natural gas in the industrial, commercial, and residential sectors. At present, Cyprus neither produces nor consumes any natural gas, nor is the country an oil producer. However, Cyprus plans to begin natural gas production from the offshore Aphrodite field as early as 2017. EIA estimates petroleum products met up to 98 percent of Cyprus' total primary energy demand in 2011, so the effect of oil prices on the country's economy is significant. Consumption of petroleum averaged 55,000 bbl/d between 2000 and 2011, peaking in 2008 at 60,000 bbl/d.

Jordan

With limited hydrocarbon resources, domestic sources of oil and natural gas met just 3 percent of Jordan's energy demand in 2011. Government statistics indicate that in 2011 the use of oil and oil products accounted for over 80 percent of Jordan's total primary energy demand. Over the past several decades Jordan produced nominal quantities of oil, and production has been in decline since peaking at just 1,000 bbl/d in 1986. In 2012, production was effectively zero. Jordan plans to begin producing and utilizing its oil shale resources to power a 500-megawatt electric plant, which could begin operations as soon as 2017. Prospects for additional oil production are poor in the short term, but Jordan's natural gas sector shows some potential for growth.

The most promising potential for additional domestic natural gas production is from BP's activities at Jordan's Risha field, which produced roughly 15 MMcf/d in 2012. The field already produces over half of the country's natural gas, and Jordanian officials hope to increase the field's output to over 300 MMcf/d by 2015. Domestic production of natural gas averaged 9.5 Bcf from 2000-2011, peaking in 2006 at more than 11 Bcf. Jordan's domestic production meets some internal demand, but the country continues to rely on imports to meet the majority of its natural gas requirements. After hitting a peak of 108 Bcf in 2008, Jordan's natural gas consumption fell to just 37 Bcf in 2011 as a result of interruptions to the Arab Gas Pipeline (AGP).

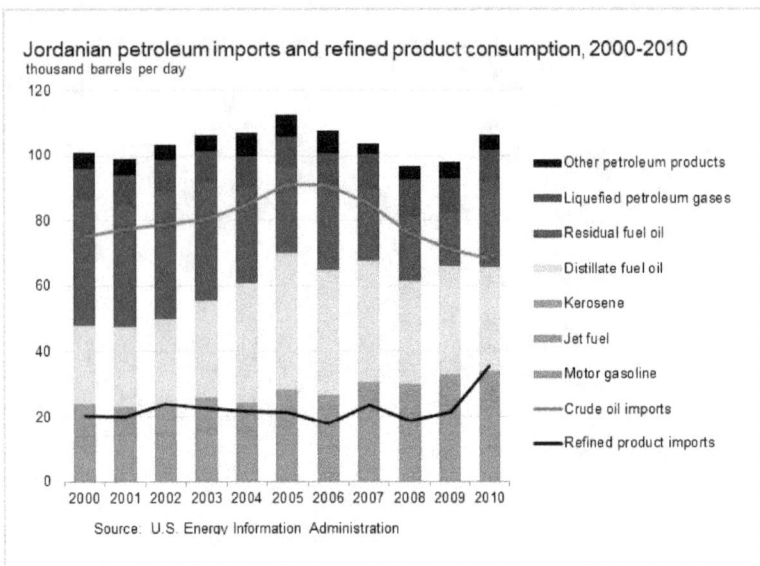

Jordanian petroleum imports and refined product consumption, 2000-2010
thousand barrels per day

Source: U.S. Energy Information Administration

Lebanon

Lebanon hopes that natural gas volumes from as-yet-undiscovered offshore fields will provide the necessary energy supply to meet domestic demand. A recent paper from Lebanon's Ministry of Energy and Water proposed boosting the share of natural gas in the energy mix to two-thirds by 2030 (natural gas is not currently a part of the country's energy mix after the loss of Egyptian supply). Unless future exploration proves as successful as that in neighboring Israel, that goal will be difficult to achieve. In 2011, Lebanon's oil demand was a record 134,000 bbl/d, up 55,000 bbl/d from just four years earlier.

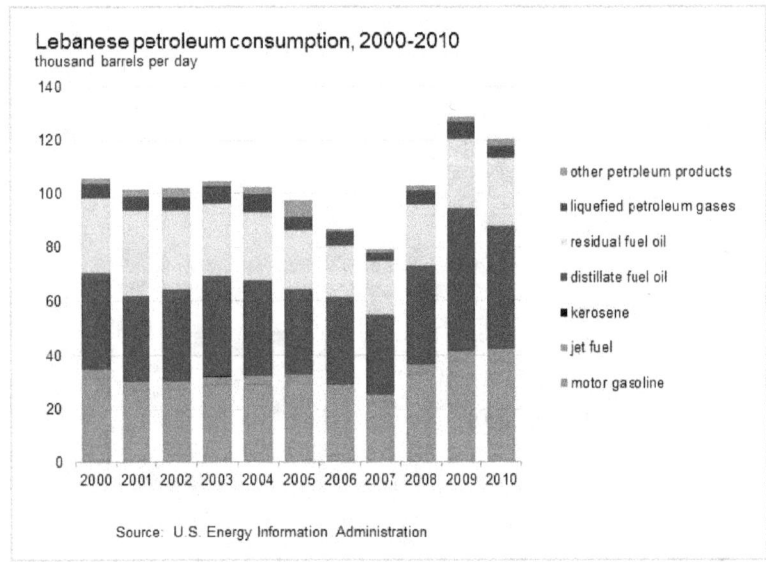

Lebanese petroleum consumption, 2000-2010
thousand barrels per day

Source: U.S. Energy Information Administration

Palestinian Territories

The Palestinian Territories currently produce neither oil nor natural gas. Petroleum products accounted for an average of 71 percent of total primary energy demand between 2000 and 2010, ranging as high as 80 percent in some years. Nevertheless, in absolute terms the Palestinian Territories' oil consumption is quite small, at just over 16,000 bbl/d in 2010.

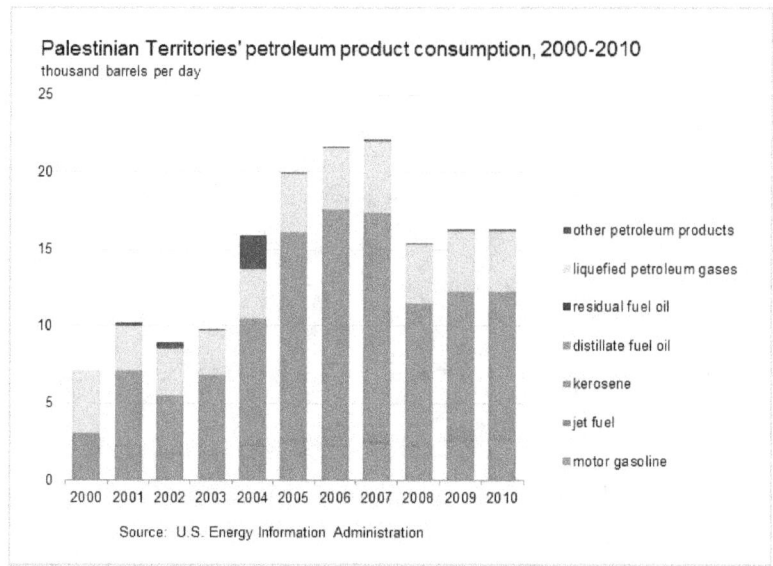

Palestinian Territories' petroleum product consumption, 2000-2010
thousand barrels per day

Legend:
- other petroleum products
- liquefied petroleum gases
- residual fuel oil
- distillate fuel oil
- kerosene
- jet fuel
- motor gasoline

Source: U.S. Energy Information Administration

Refining and processing

There are only five operating refineries in the eastern Mediterranean region, two of which are currently operating at reduced levels.

The eastern Mediterranean region's refining capabilities are insufficient to meet internal demand, leading to net imports of petroleum products to the region. Israel is the one country that is technically able to meet internal demand, but because they export some petroleum products they must import additional refined products to meet internal demand. Israel's two refineries have a combined nameplate capacity of approximately 220,000 bbl/d.

Much of Syria's crude oil is heavy and sour, making the processing and refining of the country's crudes difficult and expensive. Syria has two state-owned refineries, one in Homs and the other in Banias. The combined capacity of the two refineries at the end of 2012 was just below 240,000 bbl/d according to the Oil & Gas Journal, a total capacity that meets only three-quarters of Syria's domestic demand for refined products. With damage to pipelines and other infrastructure around the refinery at Homs in particular, Syria's actual refining capacity may be lower. In February 2013, Syria's Prime Minister indicated that the Homs and Banias refineries were running at 70 and 79.5 percent capacity, respectively. An agreement between Syria, Venezuela, Iran, and Malaysia to build a refinery with 140,000 bbl/d capacity at Furqlus, near Homs, remains a possibility.

Both Cyprus and Lebanon had operating refineries for a time. However, due to myriad economic and security issues they were forced to close. The Palestinian Territories do not currently have any refining capacity.

Refineries

Country	Refinery location	Nameplate capacity
Operational		
Israel	Ashdod	90,000
	Haifa	130,000
Jordan	Zarqa	90,400
Syria	Banias	133,000

	Homs	107,000
No longer operating		
Cyprus	Larnaca	27,000
Lebanon	Tripoli	20,000
	Zahrani	17,500

*Source: EIA estimates, IHS, Oxford Institute for Energy
Studies, Oil & Gas Journal, company reports, trade press*

Imports and exports

Exports of oil are almost nonexistent after Syria's production fell sharply with the onset of violence in 2011. No countries in the region currently export natural gas.

The eastern Mediterranean region is not currently a significant oil or natural gas exporting region. The eastern Mediterranean countries are heavily dependent on oil imports, although Syria—until recently—was able to maintain a fairly robust oil export sector. Sanctions and damage from the ongoing fighting have left the country unable to export any significant quantities of oil or petroleum products, although this had limited effects on its regional neighbors since most of Syria's exports previously went to European markets. Israel, the only exporter of petroleum products in the region, exports relatively small quantities of refined products.

Several of the countries in the eastern Mediterranean rely on imports of natural gas, although nearly all of them hope to develop domestic resources to meet domestic demand. At this point, only Cyprus and Israel appear poised to capitalize on such resources, with Israel aiming to be self-sufficient in the near future.

None of the eastern Mediterranean countries are currently exporting natural gas, however the recent discoveries in Cyprus and Israel, as well as the potential of the Levant Basin, make natural gas exports from the region a likely possibility. In fact, Cyprus recently concluded the initial stages of a proposed liquefied natural gas (LNG) liquefaction facility—located at Vasilikos—in hopes of beginning exports by 2019. Israel is also moving closer to developing the ability to export natural gas, although high projected domestic demand raises some concerns over how much natural gas the country will be able to export.

As a region, there is very little cross-border energy trade at this time. Natural gas flows from Egypt, which went to Israel, Jordan, Lebanon, and Syria at one point or another, have all but stopped, and years of conflict have left few of the region's oil pipelines in working order. A stable security environment and the development of new resources must occur before significant progress towards more intra-regional trade can take place.

Syria

Oil exports were a vital component of Syria's export economy until recently, accounting for roughly 35 percent of the country's total export revenues in 2010, according to IHS reports. In the 12 months prior to the onset of protests in March 2011, approximately 99 percent of Syria's crude exports went to Europe (including Turkey) according to trade data available to EIA. In 2012, Syria loaded only four cargoes, none of which went to European markets. In 2011, Syria exported $3.6 billion worth of oil to European markets according to news reports, so the loss of European export markets severely constrains the country's revenue stream. In April 2013, Syria's Oil Minister indicated that unauthorized exports to Turkey totaled 750,000 barrels of oil since the beginning of the conflict.

Imports of refined products to Syria appear to be ramping up in 2013, after dropping considerably as the conflict expanded. Early in the year, the Syrian government began allowing private companies to import petroleum products. This development was notable because the sanctions imposed by the United States, European Union, and others prevent international companies from dealing with Syrian state companies. Reports also indicate that Syria receives products via tanker across its border with Lebanon, but there is uncertainty over the quantities and companies involved. Sanctions, and the resulting loss of oil export revenues, make importing petroleum products difficult, although several countries continue to pursue energy deals with Syria, including Iraq, Iran, Russia, and Venezuela. The Syrian Minister of Petroleum and Mineral Resources stated in June 2013 that the country was importing roughly $500 million worth of petroleum products to meet demand, a significant jump from pre-conflict levels.

Syria does not currently possess the ability to export LNG, nor are current natural gas production levels sufficient to justify exporting volumes via pipeline. Over recent years, Syria imported natural gas from Egypt to supplement its own domestic production, but volumes dropped by more than 60 percent between 2010 and 2011 (from 24.4 Bcf to 8.8 Bcf according to Cedigaz data). Syria no longer receives natural gas from the AGP, although the infrastructure is still in place so a re-start is not inconceivable. Imports via the AGP began in 2008, and there are plans to expand the pipeline into Turkey and perhaps even Europe, but no firm project proposals exist.

Israel

Israel exports small quantities of refined products, but with domestic production being virtually nonexistent, imported oil meets nearly 99 percent of total oil demand, and over 80 percent of those imports are crude oil. Israeli exports of refined products grew from approximately 66,000 bbl/d in 2000 to 84,000 bbl/d in 2010, with residual and distillate fuel oil accounting for approximately half of exports over that period.

Largely as a result of poor regional relations, Israel does not share any international oil pipelines with its neighbors. In 2012, the majority of Israel's crude oil imports came from Russia and Azerbaijan via tanker vessels. Israel plans to reduce its dependence on oil imports through an expansion of its rapidly-growing natural gas sector.

A significant portion of Israel's natural gas over the past several years came from neighboring Egypt, but Egypt suspended supply in the aftermath of unrest beginning in 2011. The el-Arish-Ashlekon pipeline (Egypt-Israel) met up to 40 percent of Israel's demand prior to its closure, but with additional volumes from Israel's offshore fields becoming available in early 2013, the country no longer requires Egyptian supply.

In early 2013, Israel began receiving LNG cargoes on a short-term contract (two loads per month) in order to bridge the gap created by the loss of Egyptian volumes, the swift decline in production of the Mari-B field, and the start-up of the Tamar field in April 2013. The contract could deliver between 50 and 70 Bcf per year to Israel, but delivered volumes hinge on how quickly operators can bring the Tamar field up to peak capacity.

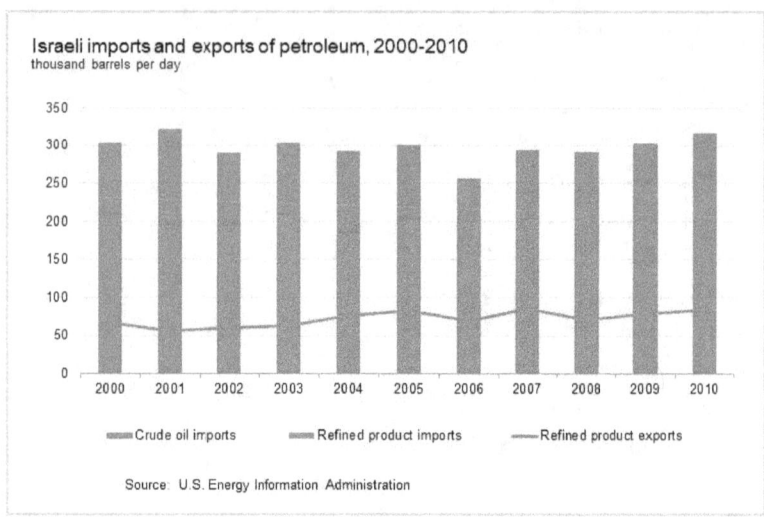

Israeli imports and exports of petroleum, 2000-2010
thousand barrels per day

Crude oil imports   Refined product imports   Refined product exports

Source: U.S. Energy Information Administration

Cyprus

Like Israel, Cyprus hopes to develop sufficient volumes of natural gas to meet domestic demand and reduce the need for imported petroleum products, but commercial development of the country's natural gas resources is still a few years away. Assuming that Cyprus completes the necessary infrastructure improvements, natural gas imports delivered on a short-term supply contract could begin in 2015. That short-term contract should provide adequate supply until volumes from the Aphrodite field are commercially available. Early reports indicate that import volumes would be in the 28-41 Bcf per year range. Given that natural gas-fired generation is still a few years away, the need to import petroleum products is unlikely to decline in the near term.

Jordan

Jordan's energy mix began shifting away from oil and oil products and towards natural gas around 2002, and the development of the Arab Gas Pipeline was critical to that shift. The shift towards natural gas reversed course as unrest in Egypt beginning in 2011 led to numerous disruptions on the pipeline, and oil and oil product imports replaced lost volumes from the AGP.

In 2010, Jordan imported approximately 68,000 barrels per day (bbl/d) of crude oil and 36,000 bbl/d of refined products. Those totals have grown over the past few years, as Jordan currently imports up to 80,000 bbl/d of crude oil from Saudi Arabia under contract and receives up to 12,500 bbl/d by tanker truck from Iraq (which it receives at a discount). A recent agreement between Jordan and Iraq could boost that total to 15,000 bbl/d in the near future. The Jordanian Department of Statistics reported in April 2013 that more than 30 percent of the country's total import bill in 2012 was for energy products.

Natural gas import volumes fell dramatically in 2011 as a result of the disruptions on the AGP, falling from 89 Bcf in 2010 to 29 Bcf in 2011. EIA estimates for 2012 indicate that volumes from the AGP fell to below 15 Bcf for the year. A new agreement between Jordan and Egypt calls for volumes to reach 250 MMcf/d (91 Bcf per year), but growing demand in Egypt will make meeting those supply targets difficult. Initial estimates indicate that Jordan boosted oil imports (particularly fuel oil, which is used in power generation) by more than 25 percent in 2011 to help make up for the loss of natural gas volumes from the AGP.

Lebanon

Without reserves or production of natural gas, Lebanon historically relied entirely on imports to meet internal demand. In 2010, Lebanon imported 120,000 bbl/d of refined oil products, which accounted for over 90 percent of total primary energy use in the country. In 2009 and 2010, Lebanon was able to import small volumes of natural gas via the AGP. The AGP promised to deliver volumes of natural gas from Egypt to Lebanon via Jordan and Syria, but disruptions are frequent and persistent largely because of unrest in Egypt and the overall security environment in the region. With limits on how much gas Egypt can export given rising demand in that country, and the crisis in neighboring Syria limiting the utility of the AGP, Lebanon is unlikely to begin importing significant volumes of natural gas in the short term.

Palestinian Territories

The Palestinian Territories import all of their energy resources. Neither the West Bank nor Gaza Strip has a refinery, so the territories must import petroleum products to meet internal demand. In recent years, most imports of refined petroleum products have been either distillate fuel oil or liquefied petroleum gases. From 2000-2010, those two products accounted for 80 percent of petroleum product consumption in the Palestinian Territories.

International energy infrastructure

The recent discoveries of natural gas and a favorable location between major supply and demand centers make the eastern Mediterranean region a frequent target of energy import and export project proposals.

The recent discoveries of natural gas in the Levant Basin re-invigorated efforts to transform the eastern Mediterranean into an energy transit hub. There are proposals to build international oil and natural gas pipelines, LNG liquefaction plants, and petroleum terminals in the eastern Mediterranean, in part as a result of the recent significant discoveries of natural gas, but also as a reflection of the region's strategic geographic location. The eastern Mediterranean's location between the major oil producers of the Middle East and major demand markets in Europe is strategically significant. Additionally, the nearby Suez Canal is a major chokepoint in international shipping, particularly for oil and oil products. Further, the large offshore discoveries of natural gas make the outlook for the region as an energy hub more promising.

At present, there is only one active major international pipeline in the eastern Mediterranean region, although there are a number of inactive and proposed pipelines that could become significant for energy transit in the next several years. The potential economic gains from energy exports are enticing, but there are outstanding issues that threaten to undermine progress towards that outcome. Moving from the discovery phase to the commercial production phase and from there to develop exporting capability requires ongoing commitment in the face of several regional issues, including both security and economic challenges. In particular, the impact of the current security environments in Egypt, Iraq, Syria, and Turkey will continue to impact the viability and attractiveness of international pipeline projects in the region.

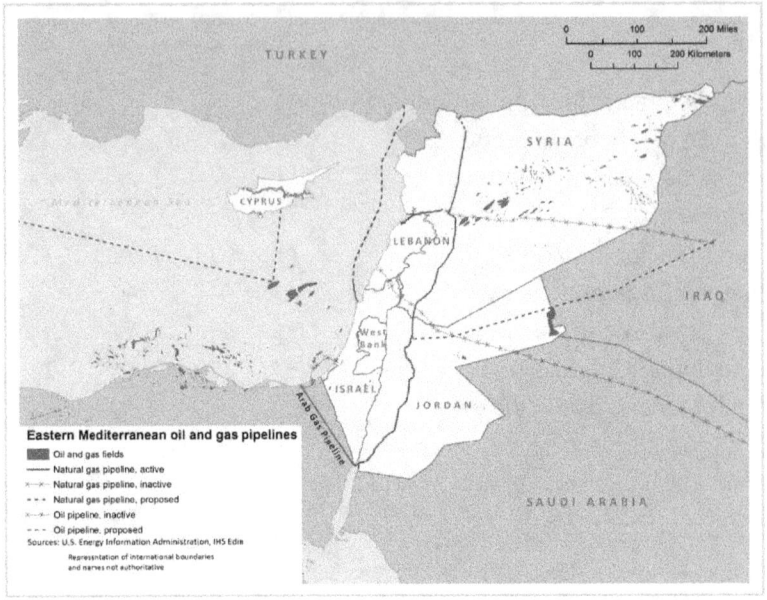

Eastern Mediterranean oil and gas pipelines

- Oil and gas fields
- Natural gas pipeline, active
- Natural gas pipeline, inactive
- Natural gas pipeline, proposed
- Oil pipeline, inactive
- Oil pipeline, proposed

Sources: U.S. Energy Information Administration, IHS Edin

Representation of international boundaries
and names not authoritative

Pipelines

The Arab Gas Pipeline (AGP) runs from el-Arish in Egypt through Jordan and into Syria. From Syria, the AGP has a spur to Lebanon, and plans call for the pipeline to eventually connect with Turkey, but ongoing hostilities in Syria make that prospect unlikely in the near term. Following interruptions during 2010 and 2011 due in large part to attacks on the pipeline in the Sinai Peninsula, flows to Jordan have stabilized, but at levels far below the contract requirements. Recent unrest in Egypt could further reduce flows. Egypt also has an export pipeline to Israel (from al-Arish to Ashkelon), but volumes were intermittent over the past several years and are not currently available.

Active, inactive, and proposed pipelines in the eastern Mediterranean

Pipelines	Capacity bbl/d	MMcf/d	Notes
Active			
Egypt-Jordan-Syria-Lebanon (Arab Gas Pipeline)	--	966	Egypt-Jordan flows intermittent and at volumes less than contracted; flows to Syria, Lebanon offline
Iraq-Syria (Ain Zalah-Sufayah-Suweidiya)	--	--	Small pipeline in the northeast of Syria; not a significant international pipeline
Inactive			
Egypt-Israel (el-Arish-Ashkelon)	--	677	No flows since 2011
Iraq-Syria (SCOTLINE), two pipelines	1,400,000	--	Iraqi sections inoperable; status of Syrian section uncertain
Saudi Arabia-Jordan (Trans-Arabian Pipeline [Tapline])	315,000-500,000	--	Section from Saudi Arabia to Jordan closed since 1990; discussions on re-opening occur occasionally
Syria-Lebanon (Gasyle 1)	--	300	Not currently in operation; temporarily supplied Arab Gas Pipeline volumes to Lebanon
Proposed			
Azerbaijan-Turkey-Syria	--	100-300	Infrastructure build-out not completed; project unlikely to move forward
Cyprus-Greece	--	unknown	Proposed export pipeline from

			Cyprus; could connect to European distribution network
Egypt-Palestinian Territories	--	unknown	Intended to supply natural gas to PT generating facilities; no details available
Iran-Iraq-Syria Pipeline (Islamic Gas Pipeline)	--	110	News reports indicate construction completed by 2013; 20-25 MMcm/d to Syria, 20-25 MMcm/d to Iraq (power)
Iraq-Jordan (Haditha-Aqaba)	1,000,000	350	Export pipeline to Red Sea; some oil and natural gas for use in Jordan
Iraq-Jordan (Zarqa spur line of Haditha-Aqaba pipeline)	98,000	--	Proposed as alternative to trucks on this route; no significant progress
Iraq-Syria (Haditha-Banias), two oil pipelines, one natural gas pipeline	2,750,000	unknown	Two oil pipelines, one from norther Iraq and one from southern Iraq; one natural gas pipeline to aid operation
Israel-Turkey	--	unknown	Preliminary discussions on Israel-Turkey natural gas pipeline as alternative to LNG exports; no project proposal as of July 2013
Syria-Lebanon (Homs-Tripoli)	--	378	Project abandoned
Syria-Turkey (Aleppo-Kilis)	--	145	Arab Gas Pipeline extension; project stalled
Turkey-Israel (Ceyhan-Haifa)	800,000	--	265 mile pipeline would connect Israel to Turkish energy hub in Ceyhan; no significant progress

Source: EIA, IHS EDIN, IHS Global Insight, PFC Energy, Pipelines International, company reports

Despite the current operating status of the AGP, additional energy sector cooperation across the region is possible, particularly with the recent discoveries of natural gas altering the supply-side outlook in the region. Policymakers hope those discoveries will help satisfy internal demand and eventually pave the way for the region to become an important energy hub. Cyprus and Israel already have plans to export newly-discovered natural gas, but determining how—and to where—remains undecided. Currently, there are proposals to build liquefied natural gas (LNG) liquefaction facilities in both Cyprus and Israel, but export pipelines remain a possibility.

Arab Gas Pipeline

Source: U.S. Energy Information Administration, IHS
Representation of international boundaries is not necessarily authoritative

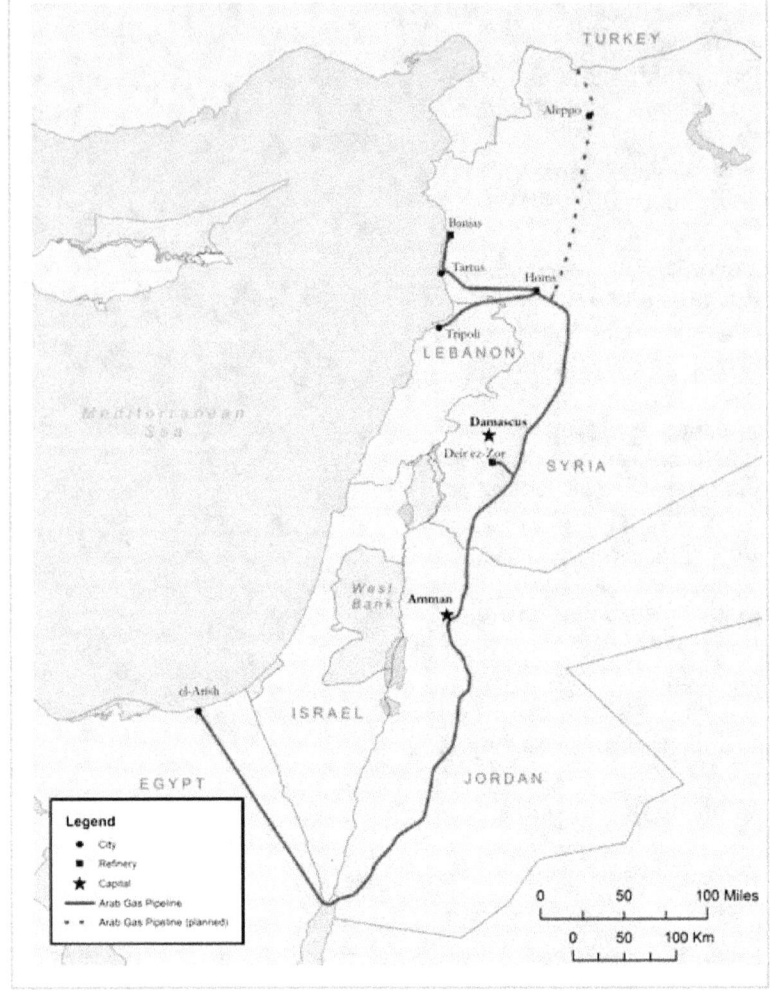

Proposed energy infrastructure

The effects of unrest in Egypt and Syria limit the use of existing international energy infrastructure in the region, but the recent offshore natural gas finds give new hope to several new international projects.

Export infrastructure

Plans to develop the region's export infrastructure are focused primarily on natural gas volumes from the Levant Basin, but there are also a few international oil projects that could become viable in the next few years.

Cyprus hopes to begin exporting natural gas from the Aphrodite field by 2019. The key to this plan is the construction of a new LNG terminal at Vasilikos. That facility could be operational as early as 2019, with construction slated to begin in 2015. Plans call for three liquefaction trains at the terminal, each capable of producing 5 million tonnes of LNG per year. Pre-front-end engineering design work on the proposed facility and an associated pipeline should conclude in 2013. Cyprus aims to incorporate offshore Israeli natural gas production as well as domestic volumes to supply the LNG facility as part of the country's broader strategy of becoming an energy hub in the region. As of May 2013, no agreements between Cyprus and Israel were in place.

There has also been talk of tying the Israeli offshore volumes into the Cyprus infrastructure being built for their LNG facility at Vasilikos, but at this time Israel appears to prefer a domestic option. The discoveries of the Tamar and Leviathan fields (among several others) should allow the country to become a significant exporter of natural gas in the next decade. There are competing proposals to build pipelines and LNG infrastructure to support natural gas exports, but deliberations about how Israel will get its natural gas to market are still ongoing. A recently-released report by the Natural Gas Inter-Ministerial Committee suggested that any development plans should guarantee Israeli supply for 25 years, exports should not exceed 500 billion cubic meters (17.7 Tcf), and any LNG export facility would be best placed within Israel.

One option is for Israel to export natural gas volumes as LNG from a floating liquefied natural gas (FLNG) installation off the Mediterranean coast. One plan, the Tamar FLNG project, is in its second phase, and could begin operations by 2017. The FLNG facility would draw on volumes from the nearby Tamar and Dalit fields and be able to export up to 3 million tonnes per year (144 Bcf per year). Estimates on the ultimate cost of this proposal are somewhere around $5 billion. Another (more expensive) option is to build an LNG facility onshore in Israel, but this option remains cost-prohibitive both in terms of construction costs and security costs during operation of the facility.

There are already plans underway to have Israeli firms supply natural gas to Jordanian industrial facilities on the coast of the Red Sea. Israel also has plans to upgrade the Eilat port on the Red Sea to 160,000 cubic meters of natural gas storage with a connection to the Ramat Yotam facility (1.2 million cubic meters of storage capacity). Given Jordan's growing demand for natural gas, an agreement on exports may occur, but political factors complicate the issue and could hinder cooperation between the two countries.

Egypt is another possible destination, as the country already has the infrastructure necessary to receive and process natural gas into LNG. Rising demand in the country means that additional volumes are necessary in the near term. Cooperation between Israel and Egypt in the natural gas sector is unlikely to occur in the short term given the deterioration of relations since the onset of unrest in 2011 in Egypt. Additionally, the el-Arish-Ashkelon pipeline already connects the two countries, and since Egypt suspended deliveries to Israel (and other countries in the region via the Arab Gas Pipeline) beginning in 2011, the pipeline remains a possibility for conversion. As with Jordan, politics will likely determine the nature of the Israel-Egypt energy relationship in the near term.

The recent improvement in relations between Turkey and Israel makes a direct natural gas pipeline between the two countries a possibility. The pipeline would probably be offshore so volumes from Cyprus (and perhaps Lebanon in time) could also feed into the pipeline. No formal arrangements were in place as of May 2013.

Following the Aphrodite discovery, and those in nearby Israeli waters, Cyprus intends to become an important energy hub in the eastern Mediterranean region. Cyprus could capitalize on its location between major supply and demand centers and the Suez Canal, which is an important oil transit chokepoint. To that end, a project by Vitol Tanks Terminals International (VTTI) to build a modern energy complex on the island's southern coast at Vasilikos is already underway, with several expansions planned for the coming years. The early phases of the project focus on building up storage capacity and a transshipment terminal that can serve as an alternative to the more than 200 annual ship-to-ship transfers that occur in the waters near Cyprus.

Phase I of the VTTI project should conclude in early 2014 and will provide 357,000 cubic meters of storage capacity. Phase II should conclude by the end of 2014, increasing the terminal's storage capacity to 643,000 cubic meters. A third phase—scheduled to increase storage capacity to over 850,000 cubic meters—is under consideration, but the cost (over $150 million) could be prohibitive.

Other potential export options include a pipeline to Greece and floating liquefied natural gas (FLNG) vessels located offshore. The pipeline to Greece would allow for direct access to European markets, but the economics of such an undertaking remain questionable, particularly with the reduction in the European Union's budget for energy infrastructure projects in the first half of 2013 and declining demand over the past several years. A FLNG vessel may be the most economically viable option in the short term, and it could serve as a temporary solution should the terminal at Vasilikos prove infeasible for any reason. Developments in Cyrpus' economy and the country's offshore exploration program will go a long way towards determining which of these options becomes a reality.

Import infrastructure

The eastern Mediterranean countries are heavily dependent on petroleum imports, and limited local production—further diminished by Syria's recent difficulties—means that the region is likely to need imports for the foreseeable future. As such, improving the region's connections with other oil-producing areas, like the Middle East, is a high priority for the region's governments.

Of the two oil pipelines between Syria and Iraq, only the relatively small Ain Zalah (Iraq)—Suweidiya (Syria) remains operational, but fighting in Syria could threaten this pipeline as well. The Kirkuk (Iraq)—Banias (Syria) pipeline sustained damage in the U.S.-led invasion of Iraq in 2003, and despite agreements pledging to repair and restart the pipeline, the current political situation makes this an unlikely possibility.

There are a number of proposed projects for oil and natural gas pipelines in Syria. One project proposes to build two oil pipelines that would send Iraqi crude to the Mediterranean coast in Syria, and from there to international markets. The first of the proposed pipelines would send heavier crudes from northern Iraq and have a capacity of 1.5 million bbl/d. The second pipeline would ship lighter grades from southern Iraqi fields along the same route as the former Haditha-Banias pipeline. Plans call for the second section to have a 1.25 million bbl/d capacity. This agreement also includes plans to develop a natural gas pipeline. The natural gas pipeline will start in southern Iraq and link up with the important energy hub of Baiji in Iraq, and extend to Baghdad and the Syrian border. It is unlikely that this proposal will make significant progress until the security situation in Syria improves.

Another proposed natural gas pipeline, originating in Azerbaijan, should have begun operations some time in 2012, but the conflict in Syria pushed potential first volumes further into the future. Initially expected to provide over 90 MMcf/d, delays in the infrastructure build-out have prevented delivery as of April 2013.

In May 2011, Iran, Iraq, and Syria completed a trilateral agreement arranging for Iranian natural gas volumes to be sent to Syria via Iraq. Despite the current political and security environment, all three countries remain interested in pursuing this project, with the Iraqi Cabinet giving its approval to the $10 billion deal in February 2013. If successful, the increased volumes from Iran could help close the supply gap that currently exists in Syria, and the additional natural gas could eventually be sent on to Jordan and Lebanon as well.

While Israel does not currently import petroleum via pipeline, there have been preliminary discussions about sending Russian oil to the Red Sea. The proposed pipeline would carry crude oil across the Black Sea to Turkey and then transit the country and exit at the export terminal at Ceyhan. From Ceyhan the oil would travel via tanker or pipeline to Israel's port at Ashkelon. Finally, the oil would transit Israel via existing infrastructure to the Eilat terminal near the Red Sea. Discussions on this project are preliminary.

Jordan is pursuing several oil and natural gas pipeline deals, notably with Iraq, to help bolster its energy security. One proposed pipeline would send Iraqi oil from Basra to Aqaba, located on the Red Sea. If constructed, the pipeline would initially carry up to 1 million bbl/d, with roughly 150,000 bbl/d available for use inside Jordan via a spur to the Zarqa refinery. The plan calls for a natural gas pipeline to run along the same route, with up to 100 MMcf/d allocated to help meet Jordanian demand. The total capacity of the pipeline will be 350 MMcf/d, but most of the volumes will power the pumping stations and power plants used to keep the oil pipeline operating. There is also a proposal to build a new oil terminal at the port of Aqaba—which would include storage for both crude oil and products—and operations could begin in late 2014.

Jordan plans to build an LNG terminal at its oil terminal at Aqaba. The pre-qualification submission deadline was May 2013, and Jordan's Ministry of Energy and Natural Resources suggests that the facility should be ready to receive first volumes in late 2014. As of April 2013, the proposal called for the use of a Floating Storage and Re-gasification Unit (FSRU) with a re-gasification output rate of nearly 500 MMcf/d. In the meantime, Jordan continues to search for partners to fulfill a short-term contract for delivery of about 150 MMcf/d to the facilities at Aqaba.

To help offset the loss of AGP volumes, Lebanon's Ministry of Energy and Water proposed building an LNG import terminal at the port of Baddawi. A pipeline would then connect the incoming volumes to the country's power plants, but there has not been a final decision as of May 2013.

Regional issues
Several ongoing issues threaten the exploration, production, and transit of energy resources in the eastern Mediterranean, especially the security environment, territorial disputes, and the macroeconomic climate.

Security environment

The conflict in Syria has severely limited the country's ability to produce, or export, oil and natural gas. With fighting intensifying in oil and natural gas producing regions in 2013, the impact on the country's energy sector will likely increase. Damage to the country's energy infrastructure has already cost billions of dollars, and the longer fighting persists the higher the rebuilding costs are likely to be. Spillover from the fighting in Syria may also affect the energy sectors in Israel, Jordan, Lebanon, and Turkey, and virtually all plans to use Syria as a transit country for energy resources are postponed indefinitely.

Other transit options—such as pipelines between Turkey and Israel—will require multilateral commitments, but relations between several of the transit countries are poor. For example, Israel and Lebanon are still technically at war, which could pose a challenge to cooperation in the energy sector.

Territorial disputes

Ongoing territorial disputes between several eastern Mediterranean countries could hinder exploration and development in the region, particularly in the offshore Levant Basin. Disputes over maritime boundaries jeopardize joint development of potential resources in the area and could limit cooperation over potential export options.

In addition to negotiating with Cyprus over potential shared resources at the Aphrodite field, Israel currently has several territorial disputes. A maritime boundary dispute between Israel and Lebanon could limit development in prospective regions of the eastern Mediterranean, as over 300 square miles in the Levant Basin remain disputed by both sides. While Lebanon and Israel continue to debate the limits of their territorial waters, Lebanon and Cyprus have an agreement over their shared maritime boundary. Nevertheless, that agreement was never approved by the Lebanese parliament because of the ongoing dispute with Israel.

There are also uncertainties surrounding Israel's Gal licensing area, as some reports indicate the area extends into Egyptian waters. The maritime boundaries have never been formally agreed to in this part of the eastern Mediterranean, and uncertainty around maritime delineation between Israel, Gaza, and Egypt limits the attractiveness of operating in the offshore Gaza area. Further complicating the issue is the fact that Egypt does not recognize a maritime boundary with Israel, only the Gaza strip. In addition to the Gaza Marine field, the Noa field is part of a larger play that crosses into the Gaza offshore area. Should commercially viable energy resources exist in Gaza's territorial waters, a utilization agreement could be necessary. Even if the political and legal hurdles surrounding Gaza's offshore areas clear up in 2013, commercial production is unlikely to begin before 2015.

Another complication which has the potential to deter investors is the Cyprus-Turkey relationship. Turkey disputes the Greek-Cypriot claim of sovereignty on the island, and maintains an autonomous Turkish Cypriot exclave on the island's northern territory. There are also simmering territorial disputes in the offshore territories near Cyprus, with Turkey objecting to the treaty signed between Cyprus and Egypt as confirmed by the United Nations Convention on the Law of the Sea (UNCLOS).

In early 2013, Turkey announced that it would begin punishing energy companies that participate in the energy sector in Cyprus. The first company reprimanded was Italian company Eni, after Turkey suspended it from its (limited) operations in the country after participating in the latest Cypriot bidding round. It remains to be seen how effective these measures will be in deterring investment and involvement in Cyprus' energy sector.

Macroeconomic environment

The health of the economies in the eastern Mediterranean region, as well as those in possible export destinations, will impact many of the plans for exports of oil and natural gas from the region.

The other critical uncertainty that will have major effects on the eastern Mediterranean energy sector concerns the national economies in the region and the economics of global and regional energy markets. Recent macroeconomic difficulties in Cyprus and the impact of the ongoing conflict in Syria on its economy are two prime examples of the types of events that can radically alter outlooks for a country's energy market. Further, global and regional macroeconomic developments will influence the demand for energy in key importing and exporting regions, thereby changing the outlook for production, consumption, and trade of energy in the eastern Mediterranean region.

The macroeconomic crisis in Cyprus threatens the viability of several proposed energy projects, specifically the plan to build an LNG liquefaction facility on the island's southern coast. While the project continues to move forward, the final investment decision (FID) will not occur until the end of 2015 at the earliest. Further deterioration of the macroeconomic climate in Cyprus could delay the FID.

Syria is another country facing difficult macroeconomic circumstances. Given the prominent role oil exports played in Syria's economy prior to the onset of violence in 2011, the ongoing fighting—and its negative impact on oil flows—poses a significant threat to government revenues. The direct and indirect costs of war to the Syrian oil industry could now be as high as $8 billion according to Syrian officials. A large portion of this total reflects the loss of Syria's oil exports because of sanctions. The European Union announced in April 2013 that it planned to lift restrictions on some investments in the oil and gas sector, and that it would begin allowing exports of Syrian oil by opposition forces. As of May 2013, there was no indication that the opposition could successfully export large quantities of oil via pipeline.

One other issue that will help shape the development of the eastern Mediterranean's energy sector is the health of European economies. Europe is one likely destination for any potential exports of natural gas from the region. If the current macroeconomic issues in Europe continue unabated, they could negatively affect demand in potential import markets such as Spain and Italy. While there are other potential export destinations—notably East Asia—Europe's proximity makes it a very attractive option.

Footnotes

[1] The models used in this survey included the U.S. Census Bureau's International Data Base (IDB), the United Nations' World Population Prospects (2010 Revision) database, the Frederick S. Pardee Center for International Futures' International Futures version 6.61, and IHS Global Insight's population forecast (August 2012).

[2] The USGS estimates are of undiscovered technically recoverable energy resources. "Mean probable undiscovered" in this case refers to the mean of the distribution of estimates for undiscovered resources. See the USGS Assessment of Undiscovered Oil and Gas Resources of the Levant Basin Province, Eastern Mediterranean.

[3] Algeria, Egypt, Libya, Morocco, and Tunisia

Notes

- Data presented in the text are the most recent available as of August 13, 2013.
- Data are EIA estimates unless otherwise noted.

Sources

- Agence France Presse

- APEX Tanker Data
- The Arab Fund
- Arab Oil & Gas Journal
- BBC World Wide Monitoring
- Bloomberg News
- BP Statistical Review
- Business Middle East
- Cedigaz
- The Center for Strategic and International Studies
- Cyprus Ministry of Commerce, Industry and Tourism
- Daily News Egypt
- The Economist
- Economist Intelligence Unit
- Energy Intelligence Group
- European Commission
- Eurostat
- FACTS Global Energy
- Financial Times
- Frederick S. Pardee Center for International Futures
- Government of Syria, Ministry of Petroleum and Natural Resources
- Gulfsands Petroleum Co.
- IHS CERA
- IHS EDIN
- IHS Global Insight
- International Energy Agency
- International Monetary Fund
- Israel Ministry of Energy and Water Resources
- Jordan Ministry of Energy and Mineral Resources
- Lebanese Republic Ministry of Energy and Water
- Lloyd's List
- Middle East Economic Survey (MEES)
- NewsBase
- Noble Energy International
- Oil & Gas Journal
- OPEC Annual Statistical Bulletin
- Oxford Business Group
- Oxford Institute for Energy Studies
- Petroleum Economist
- Platts
- PFC Energy
- Reuters
- Rystad Energy
- Syrian Arab News Agency (SANA)
- Syrian News Digest
- Syrian Petroleum Company (SPC)
- Transparency International
- United Nations, Department of Economic and Social Affairs
- United Press International
- U.S. Census Bureau
- U.S. Energy Information Administration (EIA)
- U.S. Geological Survey

- The World Bank